The Complete Air Fryer Cookbook for Beginners UK 2023

1001-Day Delicious,Foolproof & Delicious Recipes with British Measurements & Ingredients to Enjoy Perfect Meals.

Sidney Lurleen

Table of Contents

INTRODUCTION

An air fryer is a countertop cooking gadget that is similar to a convection oven, in using a heating element and a strong fan to move hot air. Without actually frying, air fryers create foods that are crispy on the exterior and moist and tender on the inside. The first air fryer was created by Philips, which they presented in 2010 at a consumer electronics trade show in Europe. The category has expanded greatly since then. According to some estimates, the United States has reportedly sold more than 25 million air fryers over the last two years. The original brand name of Philips, Air Fryer, is now used generically to refer to the entire category.

There are two primary types of air fryers available on the market right now: those with cooking baskets and those that resemble toaster ovens but have an air fryer convection element. They are available in numerous shapes, sizes, colours, and weights. Additionally, they come in a variety of price ranges, with smaller ones starting at just 40 and bigger multi-use variants costing upwards of 300. Many multi-functional appliances now offer cooking options other than air frying, such as roasting, toasting, baking, dehydrating, rotisserie, and more, thanks to the growth of models and manufacturers. For simple cleaning, certain versions come with dishwasher-safe parts.

When selecting an air fryer, it's important to think about how you'll use it, what foods you'll cook in it, how many people you'll feed, how much counter space you have, as well as how sensitive you are to heat and noise. Aesthetics are an additional consideration because an Air Fryer will probably reside on your countertop.

How does an Air Fryer work?

The air fryer is a ubiquitous kitchen appliance for frying foods like meat, pastries, and potato chips.

Heated air is blown around the dish to produce a crunchy, crispy surface.

It utilises the Maillard reaction. This is a chemical reaction between amino acids and reducing sugars that gives browned food its distinctive flavour.

Air-fried foods are marketed as a healthier alternative to deep-fried ones due to the lower fat and calorie content used in this type of cooking.

Food can be air-fried with just a tablespoon (15ml) of oil and still come out tasting and feeling like it was deep-fried.

In air fryers, convection heat is employed to cook food, resulting in an exterior that is crispy and browned and an interior that is moist and tender. Using an air fryer for cooking is quicker and less messy than either deep frying or typical oven roasting. The fact that air frying uses less oil is an additional advantage.

In air fryers, hot air from above passes through perforated baskets, wire racks, and/or ceramic plates to cook food at temperatures of about 400 degrees Fahrenheit. This initially cooks the outside while sealing in the moisture. If convenience is what you're wanting, several models include pre-programmed settings that can swiftly prepare common products. Additionally, you might prefer digital controls over analogue dials for time and temperature management (think LEDs and touchscreens).

Are Air Fryers Safe to Use?

It depends, is the succinct response. The food cooked in an air fryer can be healthier. When you prepare processed meals in an air fryer, such as chicken wings, French fries, and mozzarella sticks, they don't instantly turn into nutritious dishes. Dehydrating fresh produce can cut the fat and calorie content, as can cooking it in other ways, such as air frying chicken wings or frying brussels sprouts or cauliflower steaks. When air frying at home, you have more control over the oils that are used, allowing you to choose ones that are less likely to contain harmful trans fats than those used in restaurant kitchens.

There has been a limited amount of research on the health advantages of air frying, with varying degrees of success. According to a 2015 study, air frying can lessen the amount of a dangerous toxin created when potatoes and other starchy foods are cooked at high temperatures. According to the study, air frying potatoes instead of deep frying them in oil significantly lowers the amount of acrylamide, a substance known to raise the risk of developing cancer.

According to a different study, air-frying fish actually raises the risk of a dangerous chemical process called thermo-oxidation of cholesterol. When fish and meat are cooked at high temperatures, cholesterol undergoes thermo-oxidation. This process can result in COPs, or cholesterol oxidising products, which can be detrimental to human health. COPs have been demonstrated to be carcinogenic and are linked to chronic heart problems. This study discovered that COP levels in fish cooked in air fryers were higher than those cooked in traditional fryers, but it also suggested that the effects could be slightly reduced by including fresh herbs high in antioxidants, such as parsley and chives.

What Foods Can You Prepare in an Air Fryer?

The home chef has a wide range of options when using air fryers, from making their own hot wings to frying brussels sprouts quickly. Stick to air-frying veggies like carrots, brussels sprouts, or cauliflower steaks, baking or roasting potatoes with little to no oil, or dehydrating fruits to make your own apple chips and fruit leathers if you are seeking healthier alternatives.

Carnivores who are health-conscious can air fry salmon fillets or chicken breasts that have been spice-rubbed or lightly oiled for more taste. Remember that dry spices will fly everywhere and create a mess. Spices can be kept in their proper place with the aid of a thin covering of oil.

Doughnuts, cookies, potato or vegetable chips, fresh or frozen French fries and sweet potato fries, pizza, and burgers can all be made at home by home cooks. If you prefer convenience to anything else, utilising an air fryer instead of a standard oven will help you cook your favourite frozen foods faster and with crispier results.

Foods covered with wet batter or marinades cannot be cooked in the Air Fryer because they will drip and make a mess of the appliance. The use of air fryers for roasting whole chickens is debatable among home cooks. Before attempting to air fry a bird that weighs more than three pounds, you might wish to cut it into pieces or spatchcock it. The same is true when it comes to cooking burgers and steaks at home; some home cooks claim that it is impossible to produce meat that is anything other than well-done while others claim that it requires practise.

Several kinds of air fryers

The most common style of air fryer, known as a "basket type," looks like a peculiar coffee maker with a detachable basket inside. With this air fryer, air frying is the only option. This tutorial covers air fryers with baskets.

There are other rectangular multi-use air fryers such the June Oven, Cuisinart Air Fryer Toaster Oven, and Breville Smart-Oven. These have the appearance of toaster ovens on steroids and are capable of more than just air frying food (such as slow cooking, dehydrating, and toasting). They can hold more food in contrast to air fryers with baskets.

The first time, what to expect

Once the packaging has been opened, disassemble all removable components, including the removable basket with a grate or perforated tray at the bottom. These need to be washed and dried before first use.

Place the air fryer on a heat-resistant surface at least eight inches away from a wall. Replace the grate and basket when they are dry.

NOTE: Some manufactures recommend running the air fryer for 10 minutes before cooking in it in order to give it a chance to exhale. If there is a faint chemical odour (one guidebook referred to it as a "new appliance smell") which should only occur once, turn on the extractor fan or open the windows.

The dimensions you need

The issue is that you can only fit so much food in a basket-style air fryer. Your relationship with your air fryer will be a lot better if you accept this.

When cooking for one or two people,it is best to use an air fryer with a 1.75 to 3 litre capacity. Moreover,don't plan on having leftovers.

Even in larger air fryers (4-5 litres),food frequently needs to be cooked in batches. If a recipe is intended to serve more than two people,you'll likely need to cook it in multiple batches.

Important Points to Remember

- Always keep the grate in the basket. This allows hot air to circulate around the food and keeps it from standing in additional oil.

- Air fryers emit a sound when they are running,you can hear the fans spinning.

- It is useful to remove the basket and take a look at the cook on the food,but you must rotate the food every few minutes to achieve even browning. It is okay to do this at any time during the cooking process and there is no need to turn off the machine because it shuts off automatically when the basket is removed. Make sure the drawer is fully inserted to avoid faults. The air fryer will alert you by suddenly going silent.

- You will be surprised how rapidly food cooks! It's one of the nicest features of cooking with and air fryer. In the manual for your air fryer,there is probably a helpful table with frying times and temperatures for common foods. If there is less food in the basket,the cook time will be cut; if there is more food,the cook time will be extended.

- You might need a slightly lower temperature; many air fryer recipes call for lower temperature settings than traditional recipes. Even if this might seem dubious,believe it. A slightly lower temperature will help prevent food from being excessively black or crispy on the exterior while still ensuring that the inside is cooked through because air fryers heat up rapidly and circulate the hot air.

The benefits of Using an Air fryer

1.More healthy

The main health benefit of an air fryer is that it uses a lot less oil than a deep fryer. Additionally,a sizable amount of the used oil drains away without being assimilated by the food. You consume fewer calories and fat as a result.

The Maillard reaction,the chemical process that causes browning,is promoted by the convection technology used in these fryers. Additionally,this improves the food's appearance and flavour while lowering its fat content.

2.Crispier Food

One of the best characteristics of air fryers is their capacity to produce crispy meals without the need for oil. They achieve this by using convection-style heating to surround food in a perforated basket or on a rack with extremely hot air coming from all directions.

Air fryers are therefore perfect for making crispy French fries,onion rings,fish fingers, and other types of traditional fried cuisine.

An air fryer produces results that are crispier than those of a typical convection oven because it can cover the full surface of the food and because the frying basket allows any excess fat to drain away.

3. Quicker

Air fryers cook food far more quickly than the majority of more traditional alternative techniques because of the way they operate. The rapid frying process is facilitated by the tremendous heat generated inside the fryer which is continually circulated.

Some versions may need to be quickly heated up whilst others need no prior heating. Depending on the particular recipes,cooking times might be cut by between 30 and 50 percent when compared to using a standard oven.

4.Less muddle

Air frying is substantially cleaner than deep frying. This is due to the fact that while cooking only calls for a modest amount of oil,it is this oil that tends to generate the biggest mess.

The ideal cleaning solution for an air fryer is a soft bristle brush,dish soap,and water.

5.Secure

Air fryers are generally safer because they are independent units and because they require so little hot oil for frying. Less risk exists from spills and burns.

Machines are designed to turn off when the timer expires to prevent food from burning.

6.More adaptable

An air fryer can be used to prepare most dishes that are typically cooked in a deep fryer just as well or even better. There are numerous recipes to experiment with. Surprisingly,baked items,vegetables,and steaks all perform nicely.

7. Avoid distributing heat and aroma

Contrary to conventional ovens,air fryers retain their heat,so your kitchen doesn't get hotter when you use them; a quality that is particularly useful if you live in a smaller house or apartment.

The minimal amount of oil required meaning that none of the potent odours that result from deep frying are present.

8.Smaller in size

Air fryers are slightly larger than toasters but are still relatively small pieces of kitchen equipment. They work well in spaces where size can be an issue,like a small kitchen. They can even be utilised in an RV or camper while travelling,as well as on a campsite because they are so portable.

9.Reasonably priced

Air fryers are surprisingly affordable to purchase,especially given how practical and adaptable they are. They are typically sold by online retailers for around   50 to   150. However,I would advise avoiding the less expensive models and choosing quality even if it costs a bit more.

10. Simple to Use

Most of the time,air fryers are quite simple to use and require little supervision during cooking. Simply place the food into the basket,set the timer and temperature,and let the fryer handle the rest.

If you need any inspiration,there are several simple recipes available. I find frying veggies to be really simple and gratifying; the roasting effect makes the vegetables appetising.

Cleaning an Air Fryer

As with any home equipment, we advise you to refer to the owner's manual for specific instructions on how to take care of your air fryer, keep it clean, and keep it running efficiently. Generally speaking, in order to avoid a build-up of fat, food particles, and aromas produced during the cooking process, we advise cleaning your air fryer after each use. It is advised to do a periodic deep clean if the air fryer is used more frequently. Cleaning is simpler with models that have parts with dishwasher-safe, long-lasting non-stick coatings.

Unplug the device and allow it to completely cool before attempting to clean it. Be careful not to scratch or harm finishes while cleaning food debris or oil that has caked on. Before using your air fryer again, make sure that all of the baskets, racks, and other attachments are fully washed and dried. As with any electrical equipment, never immerse the device in water, and abide by all manufacturer instructions to prevent warranty voiding.

Avoid These Mistakes

Although doing any of the following won't cause your face to melt off, try to avoid doing them.

1.Avoid using excessive amounts of oil.

When handling that oil, be gentle! Oil gathers under the grate, but if it accumulates too much, it can spill and could start to smoke. In general, if a dish already has fat on it, you might not even need to use oil; nevertheless, vegetables benefit from a thin coating of oil because it aids in good browning.

2.Do not use cooking spray to the drawer.

Cooking spray has the potential to irreparably damage the non-stick finish on the baskets. Please read the manual that comes with your Air Fryer.

Instead, you should either toss your food in oil (which, in many circumstances, you already do) or rub it with a paper towel that has been saturated in oil in place of using cooking spray. I learned that frozen foods that had already been fried didn't need additional oil.

3.Low smoke point oil should not be used.

Olive oil has a lower smoke point, making it unsuitable for air frying. In addition to smoking at high temperatures, it can also develop a strange aftertaste. High smoke point oils,such vegetable oil,canola oil,peanut oil,and others,are the best to use.

4.Avoid packing the drawer.

Considering how much space they occupy on a tabletop; air fryers don't have a huge capacity. To achieve the best results,avoid overloading the drawer with food (the image used in marketing air fryers is quite misleading). It's quite tempting to add more potato sticks or beet shavings,but you'll find that cooking in smaller batches results in crispier food that cooks more quickly.

5.Shake the basket thoroughly,don't forget.

Shaking the basket sometimes during cooking ensures the food is evenly exposed to the heat,which results in better browning. Many recipes advise shaking the basket every five minutes. Flip larger objects,like breaded fish fillets,instead. It's not harmful to skip a step in a recipe that asks for shaking or flipping but doing so will prevent you from getting the oh-so-similar-to-fried-food outcome.

6.The hot contents of the drawer shouldn't be simply dumped into a basin.

In order to remove cooked food,use tongs or a spoon. Your basket's removable grate gathers extra oil; as a result,if you pull the grate out and tilt the basket onto a platter, the oil will also run out. This may cause burns,a mess,and greasy food.

7.Do not only rely on the Air Fryer's timer

Many air fryers with baskets have a dial that you may configure to resemble a vintage kitchen timer or the children's game Perfection. When the timer expires,a PING sounds and the device shuts down.

Five minutes passes really quickly on one of the models I used. As a result,I set the timer on my phone at the same time as on the air fryer,and guess what? The device was a couple minutes out! This is not a major concern because you can simply keep resetting the air fryer's timer until the food is cooked to your preference. But keep in mind that not all timers operate precisely.

For shorter cooking times,certain models function best when the timer is wound up to 10 or 20 minutes and then wound back down to the required cooking time.

8.The hot drawer should not be placed on a work surface.

Consider the drawer to be a hot pan. It will be hot when you remove it from the appliance,especially the bottom. Take hold of the drawer by the handle,not the other components,and place it down on a trivet or potholder if heat will damage your surface.

Chapter 1: Breakfast

Air Fryer Chickpeas

Prep Time: 2 Mins
Cook Time: 15 Mins   Serves: 1

Ingredients:

- 1 x 400g tin Chickpeas,drained and rinsed
- 1 tbsp Olive Oil
- 2 tsp Spice or Herb Seasoning

Directions:

1. Drain and rinse the chickpeas.
2. Add the oil and your choice of spices or herbs.
3. Toss the chickpeas in the oil and seasoning until they are coated.
4. Transfer to the air fryer basket and set off at 200°C,and air fry for 15 minutes, shaking two or three times.
5. The chickpeas should be hard and crispy when they are ready. If they are still a little soft,air fry them for a few more minutes. Add extra seasoning if required.

Nutritional Value (Amount per Serving):

Calories: 139; Fat: 13.52; Carb: 3.53; Protein: 0.33

Air Fryer Breakfast Potatoes

Prep Time: 10 Mins
Cook Time: 15 Mins   Serves: 2

Ingredients:

- 2 x medium/large Potatoes
- 1 tbsp Olive Oil
- 1/2 tsp Smoked Paprika
- 1/2 tsp Black Pepper
- 1/2 tsp Garlic Salt

Directions:

1. Peel and chop potatoes into 1-inch cubes. Use approximately 1 medium or large potato per serving.
2. Preheat the air fryer to 200°C for about 5 minutes
3. Rinse chopped potatoes in water and pat dry with kitchen towel.
4. Coat potatoes in oil and sprinkle seasoning over them. Stir so that they are all

covered.

5. Transfer potatoes to air fryer basket and cook for 15 minutes. Check on them at the halfway mark and give them a shake. Depending on your air fryer make they might take less or more time so keep an eye on them when you first cook them. They are ready when they are golden brown and crispy.

Nutritional Value (Amount per Serving):

Calories: 348; Fat: 7.19; Carb: 65.5; Protein: 7.66

Air Fryer Hash Browns

Prep Time: 5 Mins
Cook Time: 20 Mins   Serves: 2

Ingredients:

- 2 Potatoes
- 1 tbsp Olive Oil
- Salt

Directions:

1. Peel the potatoes and either dice or grate them.
2. Put potatoes in a bowl and cover with cold water. Let sit for at least 30 minutes. This will remove some of the starch and will result in potatoes that don't stick together when cooking. It also leads to crispier hash browns.
3. Drain the potatoes and dry with paper towels or a dishtowel. It's important to get them fairly dry.
4. Drizzle the olive oil over the potatoes and toss to combine. Sprinkle with salt,to taste.
5. Put the potatoes into the fry basket. Set the temperature to 180°C and cook for 10 minutes.
6. Shake the basket or use tongs to toss the potatoes. This ensures even browning. Cook for 10 more minutes. You might need less time,depending on how browned and crispy you want your hash browns to be.
7. Sprinkle with more salt,to taste,along with any other desired seasonings.

Nutritional Value (Amount per Serving):

Calories: 344; Fat: 7.08; Carb: 64.46; Protein: 7.45

Air Fryer Jacket Potato

Prep Time: 5 Mins
Cook Time: 20 Mins   Serves: 2

Ingredients:

- 1 Large Baking Potato
- 1/2 tbsp Olive Oil
- Salt and Pepper
- Optional toppings: butter,cheese,beans,tuna,etc.

Directions:

1. Preheat your air fryer to 200°C.
2. While the air fryer is warming up,wash your potato and slice it in half lengthwise.
3. Rub the potato halves with olive oil and season with salt and pepper.
4. Place the potato halves in the air fryer basket and cook at 200°C for 20 minutes.
5. Remove from the air fryer and add your desired toppings. Serve immediately. Enjoy!

Nutritional Value (Amount per Serving):

Calories: 189; Fat: 5.6; Carb: 31.52; Protein: 3.79

2 Ingredient Air Fryer Pizza

Prep Time: 5 Mins
Cook Time: 10 Mins   Serves: 2

Ingredients:

- 240g natural or Greek Yoghurt
- 350g Self-Raising Flour
- Grated Cheese (enough to sprinkle on 2 small pizzas)
- Pizza Sauce/Passata
- Toppings of your choice (pepperoni, pineapple,peppers,chicken etc)

Directions:

1. Mix the self-raising flour and yoghurt together (add more flour if necessary) until a dough consistency has been formed.
2. Split dough in 2.
3. Roll each one out on a floured surface.

4. Place on a bit of parchment paper in air fryer basket and cook at 200°C for 8 to 10 minutes, turning over halfway through cooking.
5. Take pizza out and add pizza sauce, grated cheese and any other toppings of your choice.
6. Return to air fryer basket and cook for a further 3 minutes.
7. Repeat with second pizza.

Nutritional Value (Amount per Serving):

Calories: 889; Fat: 8.45; Carb: 161.12; Protein: 38.49

Air Fryer Frozen Sausage Rolls

Prep Time: 1 Min
Cook Time: 18-20 Mins (or 10-12 Mins for mini sausage rolls)   Serves: 4

Ingredients:

- 4 large Frozen Sausage Rolls (or 12 mini Sausage Rolls)
- 1 beaten Egg (optional for basting)

Directions:

1. Preheat the air fryer to 180°C.
2. Lay the frozen sausage rolls in the air fryer basket, allowing a bit of space between each one. Optionally baste with some beaten egg or milk, which will help turn the pastry golden.
3. Air fry large sausage rolls for 18 to 20 minutes, and mini sausage rolls for 10 to 12 minutes. Check on the sausage rolls at the halfway mark to ensure they are not burning.
4. At the end of the cooking time, the sausage rolls should be golden brown on the outside and piping hot on the inside. If the pastry is still pale, turn the air fryer temperature up to 200°C for 1 to 2 minutes.
5. Leave to rest for a few minutes before eating.

Nutritional Value (Amount per Serving):

Calories: 130; Fat: 9.31; Carb: 3.99; Protein: 9.28

Air Fryer Roast Potatoes

Prep Time: 5 Mins
Cook Time: 25-30 Mins   Serves: 3

Ingredients:

- 1/2 tbsp Vegetable Oil
- Salt and Pepper
- 600g Potatoes

Directions:

1. Pre-heat the air fryer to 180°C.
2. Peel,wash and chop your potatoes.
3. Drizzle with the vegetable oil,salt and pepper.
4. Add to the air fryer basket.
5. Cook for 15 minutes at 180°C. Shake well.
6. If you're adding additional herbs,spices or seasonings now is the time to add these.
7. Cook for another 10 minutes at 180°C. Check. If required cook for a further 5 minutes.

Nutritional Value (Amount per Serving):

Calories: 180; Fat: 2.5; Carb: 36.43; Protein: 4.26

Air Fryer Mashed Potatoes

Prep Time: 5 Mins
Cook Time: 25 Mins   Serves: 3

Ingredients:

- 500 g Baby Potatoes (first early works too)
- 15 ml Olive Oil
- Salt and Pepper
- 20 g Butter
- 1 stalk Chives

Directions:

1. Wash and dry your potatoes.
2. Place the potatoes on a piece of tin foil
3. Cover with 15ml of olive oil,sprinkle generously with salt and pepper. Wrap the foil over the potatoes.
4. Air fryer at 200°C for 20 minutes.

5. Once the time is up ensure that the potatoes are fork tender. If not then you'll want to cook for 3-5 minutes more.
6. Once your potatoes are cooked through remove and place in a bowl.
7. Add 20g of butter and mash until smooth.
8. Season with salt and pepper.
9. Chop a stalk of chives and scatter on the top.
10. If you're serving family style then smooth the top and dab 10g of butter on top to give it a nice presentation.

Nutritional Value (Amount per Serving):

Calories: 427; Fat: 29.21; Carb: 37.18; Protein: 8.59

Air Fryer Cheese Biscuits

Prep Time: 4 Mins
Cook Time: 8-10 Mins   Serves: 6

Ingredients:

- 115 g Self-Raising flour
- 55 g Butter or Margarine
- Pinch of Salt
- 35 g Cheddar Cheese, grated
- 75 ml Semi-Skimmed Milk

Directions:

1. Mix together the self-raising flour and butter.
2. Add a pinch of salt.
3. Add grated cheddar cheese.
4. Combine well.
5. Add the semi-skimmed milk and mix.
6. Divide the mixture into 6.
7. Line the air fryer basket with parchment paper.
8. Drop the mixture inside the air fryer basket.
9. Cook at 200°C for 8-10 minutes.

Nutritional Value (Amount per Serving):

Calories: 633; Fat: 36.13; Carb: 33.12; Protein: 43.12

Air Fryer Pizza

Prep Time: 5 Mins
Cook Time: 8-10 Mins   Serves: 1

Ingredients:

- 1 Pizza Base
- 1 serving of Pizza Sauce
- Toppings of your choice - We usually go for pepperoni or nduja sausage and mozzarella
- Dried Herbs of your choice

Directions:

1. Spread the pizza sauce on the pizza base.
2. Add your toppings.
3. Sprinkle over some dried herbs (or fresh if you have them!). We freeze fresh herbs so we usually have some on hand,if not we use dried.
4. Lightly spray the air fryer basket to avoid sticking and then place the pizza inside.
5. Cook at 200°C for 8 minutes for a thin crust and 10 minutes for a deep pan/ thick crust. Check the pizza 2-3 minutes before serving,as cooking times will vary based on the size of your air fryer,and the pizza itself of course!
6. If you fancy making mini pizzas I find that these just take 5-6 minutes,which is great if you're preparing an after school snack or just fancy something extra tasty with a glass of wine at the end of a long day!

Nutritional Value (Amount per Serving):

Calories: 1547; Fat: 52.24; Carb: 195.81; Protein: 73.6

Chapter 2: Vegetables

Air Fryer Pumpkin

Prep Time: 5 Mins
Cook Time: 17 Mins   Serves: 2

Ingredients:

- 750 g Cubed Pumpkin
- 1 tbsp Extra Virgin Olive Oil
- 1 tbsp Cinnamon
- Salt and Pepper
- Extra Virgin Olive Oil Spray

Directions:

1. Peel and dice your pumpkin if you have not done so already.
2. Then place your pumpkin into a bowl with the seasoning and extra virgin olive oil. Mix well with your hands.
3. Load the pumpkin into the air fryer basket and air fry for 12 minutes at 180°C.
4. Then shake the pumpkin cubes and spray with extra virgin olive oil. Cook for a further 5 minutes at 200°C before serving.

Nutritional Value (Amount per Serving):

Calories: 2259; Fat: 193.86; Carb: 60.54; Protein: 112.42

Air Fryer Acorn Squash

Prep Time: 5 Mins
Cook Time: 15 Mins   Serves: 2

Ingredients:

- 2 Acorn Squash
- Extra Virgin Olive Oil Spray
- Sweet Acorn Squash
- 1 tsp Nutmeg
- 2 tsp Cinnamon
- 1 tbsp Honey

For Savoury Acorn Squash:
- 1 tsp Basil
- 1 tsp Oregano   • Salt and Pepper

Directions:

1. Cut the end off your acorn squash and then slice lengthways. Remove the seeds.
2. Spray the flesh with extra virgin olive oil.

3. For savoury acorn squash season with salt,pepper,basil and oregano. Then air fry for 15 minutes at 180°C.
4. For sweet acorn squash season with nutmeg and half the cinnamon and air fry for 10 minutes at 180°C
5. Then after the 10 minutes add honey to the centre of the acorn squash along with the remaining cinnamon. Air fry for a final 5 minutes at the same temperature.
6. Then sweet or savoury,do a fork test and once fork tender serve.

Nutritional Value (Amount per Serving):

Calories: 420; Fat: 3.64; Carb: 103.69; Protein: 7.48

Air Fryer Frozen Butternut Squash Cubes

Prep Time: 1 Mins
Cook Time: 18 Mins   Serves: 2

Ingredients:

- 1 kg Frozen Butternut Squash Cubes
- 1 tbsp Extra Virgin Olive Oil
- 1 tsp Coriander
- 1 tsp Sweet Paprika
- Salt and Pepper

Directions:

1. Remove frozen butternut squash cubes from the packaging and load into the air fryer basket. Air fry for 12 minutes at 160°C.
2. When the air fryer beeps,place butternut squash into a bowl with seasonings and extra virgin olive oil.
3. Remove excess water from bottom of the air fryer unit.
4. In the bowl,mix in seasonings and extra virgin olive oil with your hands or a spoon.
5. Load butternut squash back into the air fryer basket and cook for a further 6 minutes at 200°C before serving.

Nutritional Value (Amount per Serving):

Calories: 325; Fat: 3.72; Carb: 74.91; Protein: 9.33

Air Fryer Mediterranean Vegetables

Prep Time: 2 Mins
Cook Time: 12-15 Mins   Serves: 1

Ingredients:

- 500 g Bag Mediterranean Vegetables
- 1 tbsp Extra Virgin Olive Oil
- 1 tbsp Parsley
- 1 tbsp Oregano
- Salt and Pepper

Directions:

1. Pour the bag of Mediterranean Vegetables into a bowl. Add seasonings and extra virgin olive oil.
2. Mix with your hands until the vegetables are well coated with the seasoning and oil. Load the vegetables into the air fryer basket and air fry for 12 minutes at 180°C.
3. Do a fork test on the zucchini (it's the slowest cooking item) and if it is fork tender and crispy then you are done. Otherwise cook for a further 3 minutes.

Nutritional Value (Amount per Serving):

Calories: 962; Fat: 37.72; Carb: 76.74; Protein: 79.43

Air Fryer Salt And Pepper Chips

Prep Time: 10 Mins
Cook Time: 19 Mins   Serves: 4

Ingredients:

- 1 Medium Red Pepper
- 1 Medium Green Pepper
- 1 Bunch Spring Onions
- 6 Medium Potatoes
- 1 tbsp Extra Virgin Olive Oil
- 1.5 tbsp Chinese Five Spice
- Salt and Pepper
- 1 Chilli Pepper (optional)

Directions:

1. Peel and slice your potatoes and place into a mixing bowl. Add to the bowl salt, pepper,half the Chinese five spice,and half the extra virgin olive oil and then mix with your hands until the potatoes are well coated.
2. Place the chips into the air fryer basket and cook for 7 minutes at 160°C.

3. Whilst the air fryer is cooking, slice your peppers and spring onions, discarding the pepper seeds as you go.
4. Place them into your chip bowl with the rest of the Chinese five spice, extra salt and pepper and the rest of the extra virgin olive oil. Mix with your hands.
5. When the air fryer beeps, add the peppers and onions, and shake the air fryer basket.
6. Cook for another 8 minutes at 180°C then shake the air fryer basket again and make sure the chips are fork tender.
7. Then cook for a final 4 minutes at 200°C before serving.

Nutritional Value (Amount per Serving):

Calories: 466; Fat: 2.22; Carb: 102.53; Protein: 12.27

Air Fryer Parsnip Fries

Prep Time: 5 Mins
Cook Time: 17 Mins   Serves: 2

Ingredients:

- 3 Large Parsnips
- 1 tbsp Extra Virgin Olive Oil
- 1 tsp Basil
- 1 tsp Parsley
- Salt and Pepper

Directions:

1. Peel your parsnips and chop the tops off them. Then cut them into 3rds. Then slice them into equal sized parsnip fries.
2. Place the parsnip fries into a bowl with the other ingredients and mix with your hands until the parsnips are well coated.
3. Load the parsnips into the air fryer basket and air fry your parsnips for 12 minutes at 160°C, shake and then air fry for a further 5 minutes at 180°C.
4. Serve your parsnip fries with ketchup, mayonnaise or any other favourite dipping sauce.

Nutritional Value (Amount per Serving):

Calories: 189; Fat: 3.75; Carb: 34.48; Protein: 3.15

Crispy Air Fryer Broccoli

Prep Time: 2 Mins
Cook Time: 7 Mins   Serves: 2

Ingredients:

- 1 head of Broccoli
- 1 tbsp Olive Oil
- 3 Garlic cloves - crushed
- 1/2 Lemon - juice only
- A pinch Sea Salt and Black Pepper
- 20 g Parmesan Cheese - grated

Directions:

1. Mix together the olive oil,garlic,lemon juice, salt,pepper and parmesan in a bowl.
2. Add the broccoli and mix it all together so that every bit of broccoli is well covered.
3. Pour it in to the air fryer basket and cook at 180°C for 7 minutes,until crispy.

Nutritional Value (Amount per Serving):

Calories: 119; Fat: 7.44; Carb: 9.01; Protein: 5.41

Air Fryer Asparagus

Prep Time: 5 Mins
Cook Time: 5-8 Mins   Serves: 4

Ingredients:

- 1 Bunch of Asparagus
- Cooking spray
- Salt

Directions:

1. Preheat the air fryer to 200°C.
2. Trim,rinse and dry asparagus spears.
3. Lightly spray with cooking spray and sprinkle with salt.
4. Place the asparagus spears in single layer inside the air fryer basket
5. Cook for 5-8 mins (5 mins for thinner stems and 8 for thicker stems).
6. Remove from air fryer and serve.

Nutritional Value (Amount per Serving):

Calories: 54; Fat: 0.33; Carb: 10.48; Protein: 5.65

Air Fryer Cabbage

Prep Time: 5 Mins
Cook Time: 8-12 Mins   Serves: 4

Ingredients:

- 1 head Green Cabbage cored and sliced
- 1 tbsp Olive Oil
- 3/4 tsp Ground Ginger
- Salt and Pepper to taste

Directions:

1. Preheat air fryer to 190 degrees C.
2. In a bowl,combine cabbage,olive oil,ground ginger,salt and pepper.
3. Add the cabbage to the air fryer basket and air fry for 8-12 minutes,turning a couple of times during cooking.

Nutritional Value (Amount per Serving):

Calories: 79; Fat: 3.64; Carb: 11.76; Protein: 2.28

Chapter 3: Poultry

Air Fryer Chicken Thighs

Prep Time: 5 Mins
Cook Time: 20-25 Mins   Serves: 1

Ingredients:

- 1kg Chicken Thighs
- 2 tsp Season All

Directions:

1. Preheat air fryer to 200°C.
2. Pat chicken thighs dry with some kitchen paper before seasoning.
3. Put seasoned chicken thighs in the hot air fryer. Depending on the size of your air fryer you may need to do this in batches,or,if you can,use a trivet or shelf.
4. Cook for 10 minutes before turning the thighs over. Cook for a further 10 minutes. They should be crispy and cooked through - if they are not,return them to the air fryer for a further 5 minutes,or until they are cooked. The internal temperature should be 75°C.
5. Serve with your favourite side dish!

Nutritional Value (Amount per Serving):

Calories: 3358; Fat: 224.5; Carb: 145.61; Protein: 186.86

Air Fryer Piri Piri Chicken Legs

Prep Time: 5 Mins
Cook Time: 22 Mins   Serves: 4

Ingredients:

- 4 Chicken Legs
- 2 tsp Piri Piri spice mix
- 120g Piri Piri marinade sauce (approx)

Directions:

1. Add the spice mix and sauce to the raw chicken legs. Leave them to marinate for around 30 minutes.
2. Transfer to the air fryer basket and cook at 190°C for 22 minutes.
3. Turn the chicken legs at the halfway mark.
4. The chicken legs are ready when the juices run clear and the internal

temperature is 75°C - use a meat thermometer if necessary.

Calories: 345; Fat: 11.19; Carb: 4.87; Protein: 52.55

Air Fryer Chicken Breasts

Prep Time: 10 Mins
Cook Time: 20 Mins   Serves: 1

Ingredients:

- 1 Chicken Breast (increase accordingly)
- 1/2 tbsp Olive Oil
- 1/2 tsp Salt
- 1/2 tsp Pepper
- 1/2 tsp Garlic Powder (or seasoning of your choice)

Directions:

1. Preheat the air fryer at 180°C.
2. Brush or spray chicken breast with oil.
3. Season one side (the smooth side) of chicken breast.
4. Place chicken breast (smooth side down) in the air fryer basket. Season the other side.
5. Set the timer for 10 minutes.
6. After 10 minutes turn the chicken breast over and cook for a further 10 minutes to allow it to cook on both sides.
7. Check the chicken is cooked all the way through - use a meat thermometer if necessary.
8. Leave the chicken to rest for 5 minutes before serving or slicing.

Nutritional Value (Amount per Serving):

Calories: 143; Fat: 8.42; Carb: 0.82; Protein: 15.29

Air Fryer Chicken Wings

Prep Time: 5 Mins
Cook Time: 25 Mins   Serves: 4

Ingredients:

- 1 kg Chicken Wings
- 1 tbsp Olive Oil
- 1/2 tsp Garlic Powder
- 1/2 tsp Onion Powder
- 1/2 tsp Paprika
- 1/2 tsp Salt
- 1/2 tsp Black Pepper

Directions:

1. Preheat the air fryer to 180°C.
2. Prepare the chicken wings by firstly patting them dry with some kitchen roll. The drier the chicken wings are,the crispier they will come out.
3. Add the wings to a large bowl and cover with the olive oil,tossing them so that they are all covered as much as possible.
4. Add all the seasonings,coating all the wings.
5. Put the chicken wings in the air fryer. Depending on how many wings you are cooking,and the size of your air fryer,you might need to do them in batches. You can also use a rack in your air fryer to fit more in. The key thing is to make sure the wings are not touching each other so that they have room to crisp up.
6. Cook for 20 minutes,turning and shaking 2 or 3 times to ensure they cook evenly.
7. Increase the temperature to 200°C and cook for a further 5 minutes or until the skin is crispy.
8. Serve with BBQ sauce,Hot Pepper Sauce,Buffalo Sauce,etc.

Nutritional Value (Amount per Serving):

Calories: 561; Fat: 35.11; Carb: 9.28; Protein: 49.35

Air Fryer Hunters Chicken

Prep Time: 5 Mins
Cook Time: 25 Mins   Serves: 2

Ingredients:

- 2 Chicken Breasts (1 per person)
- 4 rashers of Bacon (2 per chicken piece)
- 6 tbsp BBQ sauce
- 50g Grated Cheese (cheddar,mozzarella, gouda or parmesan)

Directions:

1. Place the chicken breasts in the air fryer basket at 190°C and set the timer for 10 minutes; if you have a small air fryer basket,you might only be able to fit two at a time. Turn the chicken at the 5-minute mark.
2. After 10 minutes of cooking time,using some tongs or a fork,remove the chicken breasts and wrap each one in two rashers of bacon. To keep the rashers in place, you can use a cocktail stick.
3. Return the bacon-wrapped chicken to the air fryer basket and cook for a further 10 minutes,again turning halfway.
4. At the end of the cooking time,open the air fryer basket and brush the BBQ sauce equally over each chicken breast.
5. Sprinkle the grated cheese over the top of the BBQ sauce.
6. Air fry for a further 2 to 3 minutes or until the cheese has melted and the BBQ sauce is hot.
7. Remove from the air fryer and remove the cocktail sticks if you used them.
8. Check the chicken is cooked all the way through,either by cutting into one or using a meat thermometer.
9. Serve with your favourite side dish.

Nutritional Value (Amount per Serving):

Calories: 1803; Fat: 118.5; Carb: 3.96; Protein: 169.98

Air Fryer BBQ Chicken Breast

Prep Time: 3 Mins
Cook Time: 20 Mins   Serves: 2

Ingredients:

- 2 Chicken Breasts (1 per person)
- Salt and Pepper   • Smoked Paprika
- Garlic Salt or Garlic Powder
- 80 ml BBQ sauce • Spray Oil

Directions:

1. Spray your chicken breasts with spray oil.
2. Sprinkle over smoked paprika,garlic salt and season well with salt and pepper too. Alternatively,you can mix all the seasonings together beforehand and sprinkle on.
3. Turn the chicken over and repeat this step again.
4. Lay the chicken in the air fryer basket.   5. Cook at 180°C for 10 minutes.
6. Turn over the chicken breasts.
7. Cook at 180°C for another 8 minutes.
8. Pour over the barbecue sauce; I like to use a silicone pastry brush to ensure even coverage,but you can just use a spoon or whatever you have to hand.
9. Cook at 180°C for another 2 minutes.
10. Check the internal temperature of the chicken breast (in the thickest part) is a minimum of 74°C and then remove.
11. The chicken can be rested for 5 minutes before slicing and serving,or just serve up as a whole chicken breast alongside the rest of your dinner.

Nutritional Value (Amount per Serving):

Calories: 477; Fat: 15.95; Carb: 80.18; Protein: 20.21

Air Fryer Cajun Chicken

Prep Time: 5 Mins
Cook Time: 20 Mins   Serves: 4

Ingredients:

- 640 g Chicken Mini Fillets
- Cajun Seasoning

Directions:

1. Add the chicken to a bowl.
2. Add the Cajun seasoning and rub all over

the chicken fillets.

3. Lightly oil the air fryer basket (if desired - I use spray rapeseed oil)
4. Add your chicken mini fillets to the air fryer.
5. Cook on 200°C for 20 minutes,turning the chicken over after 10 minutes.
6. If you overload the air fryer basket a little,like me,then you'll want to give these a shake a couple of times during the 20 minutes.
7. Check the temperature before serving. Chicken should be at least 74°C internally before serving.

Nutritional Value (Amount per Serving):

Calories: 462; Fat: 18.08; Carb: 51.76; Protein: 22.3

Air Fryer Chicken Nachos

Prep Time: 5 Mins
Cook Time: 5 Mins   Serves: 1

Ingredients:

- 65 g Tortilla Chips
- 100 g Chopped Cooked Chicken (I used air fryer Cajun chicken on page 41)
- 20 g Sour Cream
- 20 g Guacamole
- 20 g Salsa
- 20 g Cheese Sauce
- 30 g Grated Cheese

Directions:

1. Layer the air fryer basket with baking paper. (Do not use aluminium foil as this will stick to the nachos and this can also sometimes be unsuitable for air frying)
2. Spread out the tortilla chips.
3. Share the sour cream,guacamole,salsa,cheese sauce and chopped chicken across the tortilla chips.
4. Add the grated cheese over the top covering as much of the dish as possible.
5. Air fry at 200°C for 5 minutes.

Nutritional Value (Amount per Serving):

Calories: 376; Fat: 15.33; Carb: 48.28; Protein: 12.56

Chapter 4: Meats

Air Fryer Steak

Prep Time: 5 Mins
Cook Time: Approx 8 Mins   Serves: 1

Ingredients:

- Sirloin Steak (or your favourite cut of steak)
- Oil (optional)   • Seasoning

Directions:

1. Take the steak out of the fridge and leave it out for at least 30 minutes so that it can get to room temperature.
2. Preheat the air fryer to 200°C.
3. If the steak is lean rub some oil on both sides of the steak and season according to taste.
4. Place in the air fryer - either on a trivet or directly on the base of the air fryer basket.
5. Set the air fryer timer to your desired time,depending on how well you want it cooked.
6. Turn the steak over halfway through.
7. At the end of the cooking time check the steak is cooked to your liking,remove it from the air fryer and leave it to rest for at least 5 minutes.

Nutritional Value (Amount per Serving):

Calories: 795; Fat: 40.15; Carb: 1.68; Protein: 91.76

Air Fryer Sausages

Prep Time: 3 Mins
Cook Time: 10 Mins   Serves: 8

Ingredients:

- 8 Sausages

Directions:

1. Preheat the air fryer to 180°C.
2. Pierce each sausage with a knife or fork.
3. Lay sausages in the air fryer basket.
4. Cook for 10 minutes,checking on them and turning them over after 5 minutes.

Nutritional Value (Amount per Serving):

Calories: 73; Fat: 5.15; Carb: 2.79; Protein: 5.25

Air Fryer Meatballs

Prep Time: 10 Minutes
Cook Time: 6-8 Minutes   Serves: 1

Ingredients:

- 500g Lean Beef Mince
- 1 clove Garlic,crushed
- 1 tsp Dried Mixed Herbs
- 1 Egg
- 1 tbsp Breadcrumbs (optional)

Directions:

1. Mix all ingredients together until well combined.
2. Using your hands,form small round balls (this recipe makes about 16,depending on size of meatballs)
3. Place meatballs in air fryer and cook at 180°C/350F for 7 minutes. Check halfway through and turn over if necessary.
4. If you want to add a sauce,once the meatballs are cooked transfer them to an ovenproof dish/pan that will fit in the air fryer. Pour your choice of sauce on top and place container in air fryer tray. Cook at 180°C/350F for about 6-8 minutes, or until the sauce is warmed through.
5. Serve with spaghetti and melted cheese.

Nutritional Value (Amount per Serving):

Calories: 799; Fat: 38.2; Carb: 2.02; Protein: 111.76

Air Fryer Pork Chops

Prep Time: 5 Mins
Cook Time: 12 Mins   Serves: 1

Ingredients:

- 1 Pork Chop
- 1/2 tbsp Olive Oil
- 1/2 tbsp Seasoning of your choice

Directions:

1. Preheat the air fryer to 200°C.
2. Brush oil on each side of the pork chop.
3. Add seasoning and rub it in evenly all over.
4. Place pork chop in the preheated air fryer

and set the timer for 12 minutes. Turn the pork chop over at around the 6-minute mark.

5. Check the pork chop is cooked all the way through - it should be golden brown on the outside and juices should run clear.

Nutritional Value (Amount per Serving):

Calories: 402; Fat: 24.16; Carb: 2.49; Protein: 40.4

Air Fryer Bacon

Prep Time: 2 Mins
Cook Time: Varies according to type of bacon
   used   Serves: 2

Ingredients:

- 2 rashers Smoked or Streaky Bacon

Directions:

1. Preheat your air fryer to 200°C for a couple of minutes.
2. Place your bacon of choice in a single layer in your air fryer basket. It is ok if it overlaps slightly,or the edges fold over slightly.
3. You may need to repeat the cooking a couple of times if you have a lot of bacon, or a smaller air fryer basket (like I currently do!).
4. Cooking times are as follows:
   - Smoked streaky bacon rashers - 200°C - 11 minutes.
   - Smoked bacon rashers - 200°C - 10 minutes.
   - Smoked bacon medallions - 200°C - 8 minutes.

Nutritional Value (Amount per Serving):

Calories: 1456; Fat: 138.63; Carb: 29.68; Protein: 50.15

Air Fryer Mozzarella-Stuffed Meatballs

Prep Time: 10 Mins
Cook Time: 30 Mins   Serves: 4

Ingredients:

- 450 g Beef Mince
- 50 g Breadcrumbs
- 25 g Freshly Grated Parmesan Cheese
- 5 g Freshly Chopped Parsley
- 1 Large Egg
- 2 cloves Garlic,crushed
- 1 tsp Dried Oregano
- Salt
- Freshly Ground Black Pepper
- 85 g Fresh Mozzarella,cut into 16 cubes
- Marinara Sauce,for serving

Directions:

1. In a large bowl,combine beef,breadcrumbs,Parmesan,parsley,egg,garlic,and oregano. Season with salt and pepper.
2. Scoop about 2 tablespoons of meat and flatten into a patty in your hand. Place a cube of mozzarella in the centre and pinch meat up around cheese and roll into a ball. Repeat with remaining meat to make 16 total meatballs.
3. Working in batches as needed,place meatballs in basket of air fryer and cook at 190°C for 12 minutes.
4. Serve with warmed marinara.

Nutritional Value (Amount per Serving):

Calories: 626; Fat: 29.09; Carb: 10.56; Protein: 79.19

Crispy Air Fryer Bacon

Prep Time: 5 Mins
Cook Time: 10 Mins   Serves: 8

Ingredients:

- 340 g thick-cut Bacon

Directions:

1. Lay bacon inside air fryer basket in a single layer.
2. Set air fryer to 200°C and cook until crispy, about 10 minutes. (You can check halfway through and rearrange slices with tongs.)

Nutritional Value (Amount per Serving):

Calories: 132; Fat: 12.55; Carb: 2.69; Protein: 4.54

Air Fryer Sirloin Steak

Prep Time: 5 Mins
Cook Time: 10-12 Mins   Serves: 2

Ingredients:

- 2 Sirloin Steak
- 1 tbsp Steak Rub
- Salt to taste
- 2 tsp Olive Oil

Directions:

1. Pat the steaks dry with a paper towel.
2. Brush all the sides lightly with olive oil then sprinkle the steak rub all over the steaks ensuring all sides are covered in the rub.
3. Arrange the steaks in the air fryer basket in a single layer.
4. Set air fryer to 200°C and air fry sirloin steak for 10-12 minutes. Flip the steak with tongs halfway through cooking.
5. Bring them out of the basket and leave them to rest for a few minutes before cutting into them.

Nutritional Value (Amount per Serving):

Calories: 1409; Fat: 86.98; Carb: 0; Protein: 146.03

Frozen Steak in an Air Fryer

Prep Time: 3 Mins
Cook Time: 16 Mins   Serves: 2

Ingredients:

- 2 Frozen Steak (rib eye,sirloin,etc)
- 1/2 tsp Parsley
- 1 tspBlack pepper
- 1/2 tsp Ginger
- Salt to taste
- 1 tsp Olive Oil

Directions:

1. Remove frozen steaks from their package and load them into the air fryer basket.
2. Brush the top of the steaks with olive oil then season with half the seasoning mix. Be sure to cover the edges and spread out evenly to avoid salt concentration in some parts of the frozen steak.
3. Fli p the steaks,brush with olive oil,and season with the remaining seasoning mix.
4. Turn on the air fryer and set it to a temperature of 200°C.
5. Air fry steaks for 8 minutes and turn them over using tongs. Air fry at the same temperature for another 8 minutes.
6. (This temperature is set for a well-done steak cook level. See the cooking time guide below for other doneness level)
7. If using garlic herb butter,now is the time to add it to the steaks.
8. Bring out the steaks and let them sit for another 3-5 minutes before cutting into them - this locks in the juices and gives them time to redistribute.
9. Cut and serve

Nutritional Value (Amount per Serving):

Calories: 491; Fat: 34; Carb: 1; Protein: 46

Chapter 5: Wraps and Sandwiches

Air Fryer Prawn Toast

Prep Time: 5 Mins
Cook Time: 8 Mins   Serves: 2

Ingredients:

- 100 g of cooked King prawns
- 3 pieces of Bread
- 1/4 thumb sized piece of Ginger (peeled with a spoon)
- 1 clove of Garlic peeled
- 30 g Egg Whites
- 1 Egg
- A pinch of Sugar
- 1 Spring Onion
- 1 tsp Light Soy Sauce
- Spray Oil
- 30 g Sesame Seeds

Directions:

1. In a blender combine together the prawns,peeled ginger,garlic,egg whites,sugar, spring onions and light soy sauce.
2. Blitz for a few seconds until you have a thick paste.
3. Spread this paste onto one side of each of the pieces of bread.
4. Spread the sesame seeds on to the top of the paste lined bread.
5. Add a little spray oil.
6. Spray the air fryer basket with a little spray oil.
7. Slice the bread into four triangles by cutting diagonally top left to bottom right, then top right to bottom left.
8. Place the bread in the air fryer,I personally cook 6-8 triangles at a time to ensure lots of room for air circulation.
9. Cook at 200°C for 7-8 minutes. Check at 6 minutes to ensure they do not burn.
10. Cook all of the pieces.
11. Serve with a di pping sauce of your choice,I love sweet and sour sauce or sweet chilli sauce.

Nutritional Value (Amount per Serving):

Calories: 322; Fat: 18.6; Carb: 24.23; Protein: 15.23

Air Fryer Sausage Rolls

Prep Time: 8 Mins
Cook Time: 9 Mins   Serves: 22

Ingredients:

- 375 g sheet of Ready Rolled Puff Pastry
- 454 g Sausage Meat (standard sized tube in the UK)
- 1 Medium Egg
- 30 g Sesame Seeds (optional)

Directions:

1. Remove the sausage meat from the tube and work it a little in a bowl until you have a more workable mix. You can add some additional seasoning here if your sausage meat is not already seasoned.
2. Lay out your sheet of puff pastry.
3. Place the sausage meat on the puff pastry and then roll over onto itself to cover the sausage meat. I find that I can make two batches of sausage rolls if I go widthways along the pastry,near the bottom and near the top.
4. Crack the egg into a bowl and whisk well.
5. Brush the beaten egg over the top of the rolled pastry with the sausage meat inside.
6. Sprinkle the sesame seeds over the top of the brushed pastry (if using).
7. Cut the sausage rolls to your desired size. I was able to get 22 mini sausage rolls from the mix,ideal for serving up at a party or when you have guests dropping in.
8. Air fry at 180°C for 8 minutes,or until golden brown.
9. Serve with tomato ketchup or your choice of dipping sauce.

Nutritional Value (Amount per Serving):

Calories: 158; Fat: 11.27; Carb: 9.89; Protein: 5.6

Air Fryer Hot Dogs

Prep Time: 5 Mins
Cook Time: 10 Mins   Serves: 6

Ingredients:

- 6 Hot Dogs   • 6 Hot Dog Buns

Directions:

1. Place hot dogs in basket of air fryer. Cook at 200°C for 4 minutes. Remove from basket.
2. Place buns in basket and cook at 200°C for 2 minutes to toast them,if desired.
3. Place hot dogs in buns and top with desired toppings.

Nutritional Value (Amount per Serving):

Calories: 345; Fat: 18.4; Carb: 26.15; Protein: 17.87

Air-Fried Crispy Camembert Wedges with Cranberry Sauce

Prep Time: 5 Mins
Cook Time: 20 Mins   Serves: 4

Ingredients:

- 1 x 200g pack Camembert (or Brie),cut into 10-12 wedges
- 50g Plain Flour (can be gluten-free)
- 1 Egg,beaten
- 60g Breadcrumbs (can be gluten-free)
- Black Pepper and Salt
- 1 x 200g jar Cranberry Sauce
- 1 tbsp Dry Red Wine

Directions:

1. Place the flour on one plate,beaten egg in a bowl and the breadcrumbs mixed with seasoning in another bowl.
2. For each slice of Camembert or Brie,roll in the flour to coat,then di p well in the egg,then finally roll in the breadcrumbs to coat then set aside.
3. Once all have been prepared,place 6 each into each basket of your air fryer. Set to 200°C and 12 minutes to cook on the
4. Meanwhile place the cranberry sauce and wine in a pan and heat on a medium heat for 5 minutes then remove,leave to cool and place in a serving bowl.

5. Once the wedges are nice and golden,remove and serve on a plate with the dip. Enjoy!

Nutritional Value (Amount per Serving):

Calories: 140; Fat: 2.94; Carb: 23.38; Protein: 4.92

Fish Finger Sandwiches with Fresh Tartare Sauce

Prep Time: 15 Mins
Cook Time: 18-25 Mins   Serves: 4

Ingredients:

For the Fish Fingers:
- 400g Skinless Chunky Cod
- 25g Plain Flour   • 1 Egg,beaten
- 75g Dried Breadcrumbs
- 1tbsp Olive Oil   • Vegetable Spray Oil

For the Tartare Sauce:
- 50g Capers   • 80g Gherkins,chopped
- 5g small bunch Dill,chopped
- 1 tbsp Chopped Parsley   • 1/2 Lemon,juice only
- 100g good quality Mayonnaise

To Serve:
- 8 Thick Slices of Bread   • 30g Butter   • 50g Iceberg Lettuce,shredded

Directions:

1. Cut the fish into 12 evenly sized fingers then place the flour,egg and breadcrumbs into three shallow bowls. Drizzle a tbsp of oil over the breadcrumbs and mix well with your hands,rubbing the oil into the crumbs. Season the flour with salt and black pepper.
2. To prepare the fish fingers,dust the fish in the flour,dip into the egg,then press into the breadcrumbs. The fish fingers should be fully coated in the crumbs.
3. When ready to cook,spray the fish fingers fully with oil then place on two air flow racks lined with parchment paper and insert on the top and middle shelves of the air fryer. Set the air fryer temperature to 180°C and cook for 15-18 minutes,rotating the trays halfway through cooking for even browning.
4. Meanwhile,to make the tartare sauce place the capers,gherkins,dill and parsley into a small food processor and blitz for a few seconds until chopped (alternatively finely chop the ingredients on a board with a knife). Transfer the chopped ingredients to a mixing bowl with the lemon juice and mayonnaise,season with salt and pepper then stir to combine.
5. To assemble the sandwiches,butter the bread and divide the lettuce between four slices then top with 3 fish fingers per portion and a dollop of tartar sauce,

followed by the remaining bread. Cut in half to serve.

Nutritional Value (Amount per Serving):

Calories: 615; Fat: 27.39; Carb: 40.69; Protein: 50.51

Ham Hock and Spring Greens Hash

Prep Time: 10 Mins
Cook Time: 35 Mins   Serves: 4

Ingredients:

- 600g Red Potatoes,peeled and diced into 3cm chunks
- 30g Butter
- 1 Small Leek,sliced
- 2 cloves Garlic,crushed
- 240g Sliced Spring Greens
- 25g Plain Flour
- 200ml Hot Chicken Stock
- 300ml Crème Fraîche
- 1 tbsp Dijon Mustard
- 180g Ham Hock
- 40g grated Parmesan Cheese

Directions:

1. Fill a large saucepan with water and bring to the boil. Once boiling,pop the potatoes into the pan and cook for 10 minutes,until just tender. Drain in a colander and set to one side.
2. Put the butter in a small roasting tin (approximately 23cm square),place on the middle shelf of the air fryer and set the temperature to 180°C for 2-3 minutes, until the butter has melted.
3. Next add the leeks,cook for 5 more minutes,then add the garlic and spring greens and give a stir to coat everything in the butter. Continue to cook 2-3 mins until the cabbage has wilted down.
4. Stir in the flour to the leeks and cabbage,cook out the flour for 2 minutes,then pour in the stock,crème fraîche and the mustard. Stir until everything is mixed together.
5. Gently fold in the ham hock with half of the potatoes,season to taste with a good pinch of salt and pepper.
6. Transfer the filling into an oven proof dish (approximately 23cm x 5°Cm deep) and distribute the rest of the potatoes on top of the creamy filling. Sprinkle the parmesan all over the top,then put on the middle shelf of the air fryer and cook for a further 10-15 minutes at 180°C,until the topping is golden and the filling is bubbling.

Nutritional Value (Amount per Serving):

Calories: 723; Fat: 29.96; Carb: 76.41; Protein: 41.82

Chapter 6: Casseroles, Frittatas, and Quiches

Cheesy Masala Omelette Quesadilla

Prep Time: 5 Mins
Cook Time: 5 Mins   Serves: 2

Ingredients:

- 4 Eggs
- 1/2 Onion,finely diced
- 1 clove of Garlic,sliced finely
- 1 - 2 Green Chillies,finely chopped,adjust quantity to taste
- Small Handful Fresh Coriander,finely chopped
- 1/4 tsp Ground Coriander (optional)
- 1/4 tsp Ground Cumin (optional)
- 1/4 tsp Ground Turmeric
- 1/2 tsp Red Chilli Powder
- 1/2 tsp Salt,or to taste
- 1/2 tsp Black Pepper (optional)

- 2 tbsp Milk (optional)
- 2 tbsp Ghee or Butter
- 4 tbsp Cheddar,grated
- 4 Tortillas

Directions:

1. In a bowl,beat the eggs,then add all the other ingredients minus the ghee
2. In a wide,non-stick frying pan,heat the ghee or butter over a medium heat.
3. Add half the egg mixture to the pan and leave to set,before flipping to cook the other side.
4. Transfer the omelette from the pan on to a plate and keep warm. Repeat for the second omelette.
5. Preheat the air fryer.
6. Add tortilla to the air fryer.
7. Add omelette and sprinkle over cheese.
8. Top with another tortilla.
9. Weigh down with a metal trivet or secure with toothpicks.
10. Air fry at 180°C for 5 minutes.

Nutritional Value (Amount per Serving):

Calories: 924; Fat: 54.47; Carb: 65.33; Protein: 42.96

Air Fryer Cheese Flan

Prep Time: 10 Mins
Cook Time: 17 Mins   Serves: 8

Ingredients:

- Air Fryer Pie Crust
- 1/2 Small Onion,diced • 4 Large Eggs
- 120 ml SemiSkimmed Milk
- 180 g Grated Cheese
- 2 tsp Parsley   • Salt and Pepper

Directions:

1. Make your shortcrust pastry and then roll it out and add it to your tart tin.
2. Fork the bottom of the pastry to let it breathe.
3. Then add sliced onion to the bottom of the flan.
4. Mix your eggs,milk and seasoning with a fork.
5. Add the cheese and mix well.
6. Pour the cheese and egg mixture over the onions and then place the cheese flan into the air fryer.
7. Cook your cheese flan for 17 minutes at 160°C or until a cocktail stick comes out clean.
8.Then slice into squares like school dinner flan.

Nutritional Value (Amount per Serving):

Calories: 218; Fat: 14.32; Carb: 14.11; Protein: 8.23

Air Fryer Tortilla De Patatas (Spanish Omelette)

Prep Time: 6 Mins
Cook Time: 44 Mins   Serves: 8

Ingredients:

- 500 g Baby Potatoes   • 6 Large Eggs
- 2 tsp Extra Virgin Olive Oil
- Extra Virgin Olive Oil Spray • Sea Salt

Directions:

1. Chop your baby potatoes into medium slices,keeping the skin on them. Place the potatoes into a bowl and toss them in extra virgin olive oil and salt.
2. Load the potatoes into the air fryer basket and cook for 17 minutes at 180°C.

3. In a jug add your eggs,a little sea salt and mix with a fork.
4. When the air fryer beeps,place potatoes into a silicone baking pan and pour over the egg mixture,making sure all the potatoes are well covered with the egg batter.
5. Place the silicone pan into the air fryer basket and cook for 17 minutes at 160°C,followed by 5 minutes at 180°C to ensure its cooked in the middle and the eggs have set.
6. Turn the potato omelette over,spray with extra virgin olive oil and cook for a further 5 minutes at 180°C.
7. Then slice your Spanish omelette and serve.

Nutritional Value (Amount per Serving):

Calories: 109; Fat: 5.63; Carb: 11.38; Protein: 3.29

Air Fryer Frozen Falafel Bowl

Prep Time: 5 Mins
Cook Time: 18 Mins   Serves: 2

Ingredients:

- 15 Frozen Falafel Balls
- 1/2 Yellow Pepper   • 1/2 Red Pepper
- 1/2 Medium Courgette
- 1/2 can Drained Chickpeas• 2 tsp Cumin
- 2 tsp Coriander   • Sliced Tomatoes

For the Greek Dip:
- 6 tbsp Greek Yoghurt,heaped
- 1 tbsp Fresh Mint,shredded
- 1/4 Cucumber,cut into small chunks
- 1/4 tsp Garlic Puree   • 2 tsp Lemon Juice   • 1 tsp Dill

Directions:

1. Slice and dice your vegetables and toss them in half the coriander and cumin and season them with salt and pepper.
2. Load the vegetables into the air fryer with the frozen falafels and cook for 8 minutes at 180°C. Shake and then air fry for a further 3 minutes at the same temperature.
3. Once cooked remove from the air fryer and place into a bowl.
4. Season drained chickpeas in the rest of the cumin and coriander and season with salt and pepper. Air fry for 6 minutes at 180°C. Whilst the chickpeas are being air fried put your Greek dip ingredients into a bowl and mix well. Load the dip and sliced tomatoes into your falafel bowl.
5. When they are done,add the chickpeas to the falafel bowl and serve

Nutritional Value (Amount per Serving):

Calories: 181; Fat: 3.46; Carb: 24.06; Protein: 15.42

Chapter 7: Appetizers and Snacks

Air Fryer Burger

Prep Time: 5 Mins
Cook Time: 8 Mins   Serves: 2

Ingredients:

- 2 Burger Patties - fresh or frozen
- 1/2 Onion,chopped
- 2 Burger Baps
- 2 Slices Cheese (optional)
- 2 Lettuce Leaves (optional)
- 1 Tomato,sliced

Directions:

1. Lay the burger patties in the air fryer basket.
   If you want to cook the onion at the same time you can also add these now.
2. Set the air fryer off at 180°C for 8 minutes.
3. At the 4-minute mark,fli p the burger over.
4. At the 8-minute mark check whether the burger is cooked through,the juices should run clear.
5. If you want to turn it into a cheeseburger,lay the slices of cheese over each burger. You can also lightly toast the burger baps at the same time by inserting a trivet and laying them on top of it.
6. Air fry for a further minute,or until the cheese has melted and the baps are lightly toasted.
7. Assemble the burgers in the baps with your choice of salad and sauces.

Nutritional Value (Amount per Serving):

Calories: 1177; Fat: 82.27; Carb: 13.89; Protein: 90.43

Air Fryer Sweet Potato Wedges

Prep Time: 10 Mins
Cook Time: 20 Mins   Serves: 4

Ingredients:

- 4 large Sweet Potatoes
- 1 tbsp Oil (I use olive oil)
- 1 tsp Smoked Paprika
- 1 tsp Garlic Powder
- Salt and Pepper,according to taste

Directions:

1. Preheat the air fryer to 200°C.
2. Prepare the sweet potatoes by chopping off the ends and cleaning them. Slice them lengthwise into similar-sized wedges.
3. Drizzle with oil and add seasoning. Toss the sweet potato wedges in the oil and seasoning,ensuring they are all coated.
4. Transfer to the air fryer basket and set the timer for 20 minutes. Check on them at the halfway mark to shake them.
5. After 20 minutes they should be crispy on the outside and soft and fluffy on the inside. If they are not,return them to the air fryer and continue cooking,checking on them after 2 minutes.
6. Serve the sweet potato wedges as a side dish or with your favourite dip.

Nutritional Value (Amount per Serving):

Calories: 323; Fat: 3.83; Carb: 66.4; Protein: 7.89

Air Fryer Potato Slices

Prep Time: 5 Mins
Cook Time: 18-20 Mins   Serves: 4

Ingredients:

- 4 Large Potatoes
- 1 tbsp Olive Oil
- 1 tsp Garlic Granules
- 1 tsp Dried Mixed Herbs
- 1/2 tsp Salt

Directions:

1. Wash and cut the potatoes into 1/2 cm slices.
2. Put the sliced potatoes in a pot of water.
3. Once all the potatoes have been sliced,drain the water and pat the potatoes dry with kitchen paper or a clean kitchen towel.
4. Add the oil,garlic,herbs and salt to the dry sliced potatoes,tossing them about until they are all coated.
5. Transfer the sliced potatoes to the air fryer basket and cook at 200°C for 18 minutes,shaking halfway through. The potato slices should be crispy on the outside and soft on the inside. If they are not,return to the air fryer for a further two minutes.
6. Serve as a side dish or as a snack.

Nutritional Value (Amount per Serving):

Calories: 315; Fat: 3.71; Carb: 64.7; Protein: 7.5

Air Fryer Tofu

Prep Time: 10 Mins
Cook Time: 10 Mins   Serves: 4

Ingredients:

- 300g Firm Tofu
- 2 tbsp Soy Sauce
- 2 tsp Sesame Oil
- 2 tsp Seasoning
- 2 tbsp Cornflour

Directions:

1. Cut the tofu into 1 inch size cubes using a sharp knife or kitchen scissors.
2. Place in a bowl and add the remaining ingredients,tossing everything together until the tofu is well coated.
3. Leave the tofu to marinate for 5 to 10 minutes. During this time,you can preheat the air fryer at 200°C.
4. Transfer the marinated tofu to the air fryer basket and cook for 10 minutes. Shake the basket at 5 minutes to ensure the tofu is crispy all over.
5. Serve alone or with your favourite dip.

Nutritional Value (Amount per Serving):

Calories: 156; Fat: 10.23; Carb: 6.01; Protein: 12.47

Air Fryer Boiled Eggs

Prep Time: 1 Min
Cook Time: 8-12 Mins   Serves: 1

Ingredients:

- 4 Eggs (cook as many as you need)

Directions:

1. Add room temperature eggs to the basket of your air fryer and leave some space between them so that there is room for the hot air to circulate. Use a metal rack if needed to fit more in.
2. Set the air fryer temperature at 150°C. Cook according to how well done you want your eggs (starting at 8 minutes for runny,up to 12 minutes for hard boiled).
3. At the end of the cooking time remove from the air fryer basket and plunge

into an ice bath or into a bowl of cold water - this will prevent the eggs from continuing to cook.

4. Once they have cooled down a little and can be handled,remove the shell

Calories: 1086; Fat: 71.54; Carb: 81.36; Protein: 32.68

Air Fryer Halloumi

Prep Time: 2 Mins
Cook Time: 8-10 Mins   Serves: 8

Ingredients:

- 225g Halloumi
- 1 tbsp Olive Oil
- 1/2 tsp Dried Thyme (optional)

Directions:

1. Preheat the air fryer to 200°C.
2. Slice halloumi and brush with oil on both sides. Sprinkle with seasoning if using.
3. Transfer halloumi slices to the air fryer basket and air fry for 8 to 10 minutes,turning over halfway.
4. The halloumi is ready when it has softened and is beginning to turn brown around the edges.

Nutritional Value (Amount per Serving):

Calories: 97; Fat: 7.66; Carb: 2.47; Protein: 4.62

Air Fryer Chicken Nuggets

Prep Time: 10 Mins
Cook Time: 8 Mins   Serves: 4

Ingredients:

- 3-4 Boneless Chicken Breasts
- 2 Eggs,beaten
- 100g Breadcrumbs,(approx)
- Seasoning of your choice,eg; 1tsp smoked paprika,1tsp garlic granules,1/2 tsp salt,1/2 tsp pepper.

Directions:

1. Cut chicken breasts up into small chicken

nugget-sized chunks.

2. Set up a three bowls. Add the beaten egg to one bowl, mix the seasoning with the breadcrumbs and dd to a different bowl, put the raw chicken pieces in another bowl.

3. Using kitchen tongs, di p the chicken in the beaten egg, then roll it in the seasoned breadcrumbs. Place in air fryer basket.

4. Repeat with each piece of chicken. Depending on the size of your air fryer, you may need to cook in 2 separate batches.

5. Cook at 200°C for 8 to 10 minutes. Check the chicken nuggets are cooked through before serving.

Nutritional Value (Amount per Serving):

Calories: 767; Fat: 40.24; Carb: 1.57; Protein: 94.01

Air Fryer Chicken Drumsticks

Prep Time: 5 Mins
Cook Time: 22-25 Mins   Serves: 8

Ingredients:

- 8 - 12 Chicken Drumsticks
- Seasoning
- Oil (optional)

Directions:

1. Preheat the air fryer to 200°C for 5 minutes.
2. Brush the drumsticks with some oil (optional).
3. Season the chicken drumsticks with your favourite spices. You can just use salt if you prefer.
4. Add the drumsticks to the air fryer basket. You might need to use a trivet to fit them all in, or if you have a smaller air fryer, cook them in batches.
5. Cook for 22 - 25 minutes, turning halfway through.
6. Check the chicken is cooked all the way through - they should reach 75°C internally, use a meat thermometer if possible.

Nutritional Value (Amount per Serving):

Calories: 267; Fat: 15.51; Carb: 0.25; Protein: 29.39

Air Fryer Frozen Burgers

Prep Time: 5 Mins
Cook Time: 20 Mins   Serves: 2

Ingredients:

- Cooking Spray
- 1-2 Frozen Burger Patties
- Cheese (optional)
- Lettuce,Onions,Pickles,etc. (Optional)

Directions:

1. Spray the bottom of your fry basket with some cooking spray or olive oil.
2. Add 1-2 frozen burger patties to the fry basket. Do not let them overlap each other. Just a little space between them is fine,the burgers will shrink while cooking.
3. Set the temperature to 200°C and the air fryer timer to 13 minutes and let the burgers cook.
4. After 6 minutes,remove the fry basket and flip the burgers over.
5. Replace the fry basket and let the burgers cook for the remaining 7 minutes.
6. After cooking for 13 minutes,open the fry basket and top your burger with a slice of cheese,replace the fry basket and let it sit for 1 minute. (Optional)
7. Remove the burgers from the air fryer and add your lettuce,onions,pickles,etc. (Optional) Enjoy!

Nutritional Value (Amount per Serving):

Calories: 131; Fat: 9.02; Carb: 6.12; Protein: 6.45

Air Fryer Frozen Broccoli

Prep Time: 3 Mins
Cook Time: 8-10 Mins   Serves: 2

Ingredients:

- Frozen Broccoli
- Salt and Pepper
- Garlic Powder (Optional)
- Olive Oil Spray (Optional)

Directions:

1. Preheat your air fryer at 360 degrees Fahrenheit for 2 minutes.

2. Place the frozen broccoli in the air fryer,do not allow it to thaw beforehand,do not stack them,if your fry basket is large enough,a single layer is perfect.
3. Cook the frozen broccoli at 180°C for 4 minutes. This initial cooking phase is mainly to defrost the broccoli.
4. After 4 minutes,remove the fryer basket and empty the water from the bottom of the fryer.
5. Add salt,black pepper,garlic powder (optional),and a few sprays of olive oil to the broccoli.
6. Replace the fry basket and cook for another 4 minutes at the same temperature.
7. Remove the fry basket again and add a sprinkle of parmesan cheese to top it off. Enjoy!

Nutritional Value (Amount per Serving):

Calories: 206; Fat: 15.06; Carb: 15.49; Protein: 7.53

Chapter 8: Desserts

Air Fryer Apricot and Raisin Cake

Prep Time: 10 Mins
Cook Time: 12 Mins   Serves: 8

Ingredients:

- 75g Dried Apricots
- 4 tbsp Orange Juice
- 75g Self-Raising Flour
- 40g sugar
- 1 Egg
- 75g Raisins

Directions:

1. Preheat air fryer to 160°C.
2. In a blender or food processor blend the dried apricots and juice until they are smooth.
3. In a separate bowl,mix together the sugar and flour.
4. Beat the egg. Add it to the flour and sugar. Mix together.
5. Add the apricot puree and raisins. Combine together.
6. Spray an air fryer safe baking tin with a little oil. Transfer the mixture to the tin and level off.
7. Cook in the air fryer for 12 minutes,check it at 10 minutes. Use a metal skewer to see if it is done. If need be,return the cake to the air fryer to cook for a few more minutes to brown up.
8. Allow to cool before removing from the baking tin and slicing.

Nutritional Value (Amount per Serving):

Calories: 95; Fat: 1.37; Carb: 18.8; Protein: 2.58

Air Fryer Chocolate Brownies

Prep Time: 10 Mins
Cook Time: 20-25 Mins   Serves: 16

Ingredients:

- 1 pack Brownie Mix
- 3tbsp Vegetable Oil
- 75ml Water
- 1 Medium Egg

Directions:

1. Pour the brownie mix into a bowl then

add the water,vegetable oil and egg. Mix it thoroughly and ensure the mixture doesn't have any lumps.

2. Place in a greased air fryer baking tin and spread the mixture around to get an even level throughout.

3. Set the air fryer to 160°C and let the brownies cook for 20-25 minutes. Stick a knife into the brownie and if it comes out almost clean the brownies should be ready.

4. Allow to cool then slice into squares and enjoy your air fried brownies.

Nutritional Value (Amount per Serving):

Calories: 204; Fat: 9.44; Carb: 29.74; Protein: 2.13

Air Fryer Carrot Cake

Prep Time: 10 Mins
Cook Time: 25-30 Mins   Serves: 1

Ingredients:

- 140g Soft Brown Sugar
- 2 Eggs,beaten
- 140g Butter
- 1 Orange,zest and juice
- 200g Self-Raising Flour
- 1tsp Ground Cinnamon
- 175g Grated Carrot,(approx 2 medium carrots)
- 60g Sultanas

Directions:

1. Preheat air fryer to 175°C.
2. In a bowl,cream together the butter and sugar.
3. Slowly add the beaten eggs.
4. Fold in the flour,a little bit at a time,mixing it as you go. Add the orange juice and zest,grated carrots and sultanas. Gently mix all the ingredients together.
5. Grease the baking tin and pour in the mixture.
6. Place baking tin in the air fryer basket and cook for 25-30 minutes. Check to see if the cake is cooked - use a cocktail stick or metal skewer to check if cooked,if it comes out wet then bake the cake for a little longer.
7. Remove the baking tin from the air fryer basket and allow to cool for 10 minutes before removing from the tin.

Nutritional Value (Amount per Serving):

Calories: 2647; Fat: 135.17; Carb: 314.17; Protein: 41.41

Air Fryer Pumpkin Pie

Prep Time: 10 Mins
Cook Time: 19 Mins   Serves: 8

Ingredients:

- 500 g Air Fryer Pie Crust
- 500 g Pumpkin Pie Filling

Directions:

1. Firstly,get started in making your pumpkin pie filling. I always get this started first then I can be making the pie crust as it pressure cooks. You only need 500g of cubed pumpkin to make a medium sized pie.
2. As it goes to pressure,make your pie crust. Rub the fat into the flour and sugar and gradually add in the water until you make a soft pie crust dough.
3. Spray your cake pan with extra virgin olive oil and rub it in with your hands to make the cake pan non-stick.
4. Then roll your pumpkin pie dough on a clean worktop with some flour and then cover your cake pan. Cut around the edges. When the pressure cooker beeps,mix up your pumpkin pie filling and then pour over your pie crust.
5. Place the uncooked pumpkin pie in the air fryer and then air fry for 12 minutes at 170°C and then a further 5 minutes at 160°C.
6. If you have pie crust and filling left over,then roll some out and cut ready for mini pumpkin pies.
7. Then load into the air fryer and cook for 12 minutes at 170°C.

Nutritional Value (Amount per Serving):

Calories: 527; Fat: 26.88; Carb: 74.8; Protein: 7.79

Air Fryer Pumpkin Muffins

Prep Time: 5 Mins
Cook Time: 8 Mins   Serves: 14

Ingredients:

- 150 g Cooked Air Fryer Pumpkin (see page 26)
- 2 Medium Bananas,peeled and quartered
- 2 Medium Eggs   • 175 ml Greek Yoghurt
- 120 g Gluten Free Oats
- 2 tbsp Caster Sugar

- 1 tbsp Vanilla Essence • 1 tsp Cinnamon • 1 tsp Ground Ginger
- 1 tsp Nutmeg • 1 tsp Mixed Spice • Pumpkin Seeds (optional)

Directions:

1. Load everything into the soup maker including your peeled bananas,cracked eggs and yoghurt.
2. Pulse until you have a creamy pumpkin muffin batter.
3. Pour the muffin batter into egg cups until 3/4 full.
4. Place the egg cups into the air fryer basket.
5. Sprinkle the tops with pumpkin seeds (if using).
6. Air fry your simple pumpkin muffins for 8 minutes at 180°C before serving.

Nutritional Value (Amount per Serving):

Calories: 174; Fat: 10.87; Carb: 15.17; Protein: 9.49

Air Fryer Cupcakes

Prep Time: 20 Mins
Cook Time: 12 Mins   Serves: 10

Ingredients:

- 200 g Buttercream
- 120 g Unsalted Butter
- 120 g Caster Sugar
- 120 g Self Raising Flour
- 1 tbsp Vanilla Paste
- 2 Large Eggs
- Food Colouring (optional)

Directions:

1. Place your butter and sugar into the bowl of a stand mixer and mix on speed 3 for 3 minutes.
2. Scrape the sides and add the vanilla and the eggs mix on speed 3 for a further 3 minutes.
3. Then add the flour and mix on speed 4 for 1 minute. Then scrape the edges.
4. Load the cupcake batter into paper cases to 1/4 full and then place inside small pudding dishes or ramekins.
5. Load into the air fryer and cook for 12 minutes at 160°C. Allow to fully cool on a cooling tray.
6. To colour your buttercream,place buttercream into separate dishes with food colouring if you want rainbow cupcakes.
7. Then once the cupcakes are cool,load the nozzle into the piping bag and the piping bag over a drinking glass. Add the buttercream to the piping bag and and

clip with a peg at the top. Cut the bottom off the piping bag so that the nozzle comes through. 8. Pipe the buttercream onto your cupcakes and then serve.

Nutritional Value (Amount per Serving):

Calories: 258; Fat: 16.76; Carb: 13.92; Protein: 11.85

Air Fryer Frozen Portuguese Egg Tarts

Prep Time: 1 Mins
Cook Time: 9 Mins   Serves: 4

Ingredients:

- 4 Frozen Portuguese Egg Custard Tarts

Directions:

1. Remove frozen Portuguese tarts from the packaging but keeping the foil container and place in the air fryer.
2. Make sure the egg tarts are spread out and not on top of one another.
3. Air fry for 9 minutes at 160°C before serving.

Nutritional Value (Amount per Serving):

Calories: 349; Fat: 5.44; Carb: 70.38; Protein: 5.87

Chapter 9: Sauces, Dips, and Dressings

Butterfly Cajun Chicken with Sweetcorn Salsa

Prep Time: 10 Mins
Cook Time: 30 Mins   Serves: 4

Ingredients:

- 2 large Chicken Breasts• 2 tbsp Cajun Spice
- 1 tsp Garlic Powder   • 2 tsp Olive Oil
- 1/2 Lime,juice and zest

For the Sweetcorn Salsa:

- 2 Fresh Sweetcorn
- Olive Oil Spray • 1 Large Ripe Avocado
- 2 Vine Tomatoes,deseeded and chopped
- 1 medium Red Onion,finely chopped
- 1 Jalapeo Pepper,deseeded and finely chopped
- 1 small bunch Coriander,roughly chopped
- 1/2 Lime,juice and zest
- 75g Feta Cheese

To Serve:

- 4 Flatbreads
- 1 Large Lime,cut into wedges
- 150ml Soured Cream
- Salt and Ground Black Pepper

Directions:

1. Place each chicken breast on a chopping board and,with one hand on top,cut through the breast with a sharp knife; starting at the thickest part of the chicken, but don't cut all of the way through. Open the chicken breast out and it should resemble a butterfly shape.
2. Mix the Cajun spice,garlic powder,olive oil and the juice and zest of half a lime in a bowl,then add the butterflied chicken and rub the spice mixture into both sides of the chicken. Set aside for the flavours to develop until ready to cook.
3. Insert the 10-in-1 wire rack into the air fryer with the grill plate,ridge side up, on top of the rack. Set the temperature to 190°C and preheat the grill plate for 3 minutes.
4. Spray the sweetcorn lightly with olive oil,then place on the grill plate and chargrill for 12-15 minutes,turning the sweetcorn once during cooking,then remove to a board to cool.
5. Next,place the butterfly chicken on the grill plate and cook for 15 minutes, turning halfway through,until the chicken is cooked through.
6. Whilst the chicken cooks,prepare the salsa; hold the sweetcorn upright and, using a sharp knife,cut the kernels off the corn and place in a bowl.
7. Cut the avocado in half through the centre,remove the stone,then carefully scoop out the flesh with a spoon. Dice the avocado into 1 cm pieces,then add to the bowl with the sweetcorn along with the tomatoes,red onion,jalapeo pepper,3/4

of the coriander,lime juice and zest. Season with salt and black pepper,mix well then transfer to a serving bowl. Finally,crumble over the feta before serving and the remaining 1/4 of coriander

8. When the chicken is ready,take the rack and grill plate out of the air fryer and put onto a heat proof surface to cool. Wear oven gloves to remove the wire rack and grill plate from the air fryer,as they will be very hot. Allow the chicken to rest for a few minutes before cutting into slices.

9. Place the flat breads on two airflow racks and set the air fryer temperature to 180°C for 3 minutes to warm them.

10. Serve the chicken garnished with lime wedges along with the salsa,soured cream and warm flatbreads.

Nutritional Value (Amount per Serving):

Calories: 774; Fat: 45.32; Carb: 13.75; Protein: 75.86

Chicken Satay Skewers with Coconut Sauce

Prep Time: 10 Mins
Cook Time: 18 Mins   Serves: 4

Ingredients:

- 500g Chicken Breast
- Vegetable Oil spray
- Satay Marinade
- 2cm piece Root Ginger,peeled and grated
- 1 Large Clove Garlic,crushed
- 1 tbsp Low Sodium Soy Sauce
- 1 tbsp Peanut Butter
- 50g Korma Curry Paste

For the Coconut Sauce:
- 1 clove Garlic
- 200g can Light Coconut Milk
- 1 tbsp Smooth Peanut Butter
- 2 tsp Cornflour,mixed with 2 tbsp Water
- 1 tbsp Low Sodium Soy Sauce
- 1/4 tsp Sriracha Sauce
- 1/2 Lime,juiced

To Serve:
- 300g Ready Prepared Cauliflower Rice

Directions:

1. Dice the chicken,then place all of the satay ingredients into a bowl and mix to combine. Add the chicken to the satay marinade and mix well to coat the chicken. Leave in the fridge for at least an hour,for the flavours to develop.

2. When ready to cook,thread the chicken onto 8 lightly oiled air fryer skewers.

Spray the chicken lightly with oil,then assemble and insert the skewer rack (as directed in the instruction manual). Activate the Rotisserie programme and cook the skewers for 18 minutes. Check that the chicken is piping hot before removing from the air fryer,using the rotisserie handle and oven gloves. (If you prefer,the kebabs can be cooked on a lightly oiled air flow rack at 180°C for 20-25 minutes).

3. Meanwhile to prepare the sauce,place all of the ingredients into a small saucepan and gently bring to the boil. Turn down the heat and simmer on a moderate heat for 12-15 minutes,until the sauce thickens.

4. When almost ready to serve,heat the cauliflower rice,as directed on the pack instructions.

5. Serve the skewers with a drizzle of coconut sauce and a side portion of cauliflower rice.

Nutritional Value (Amount per Serving):

Calories: 506; Fat: 30.79; Carb: 26.94; Protein: 34.3

Indian Style Cauliflower Fritters

Prep Time: 10 Mins
Cook Time: 15 Mins   Serves: 4

Ingredients:

- 1 Medium Sized Head of Cauliflower
- 1 Egg
- 1-2 tbsp Flour
- 1 tsp Curry Powder
- 1/2 tsp Turmeric
- 1 tbsp Fresh Chopped Coriander
- 1-2 cloves Garlic,minced
- 1/2 tsp Ginger Powder or Grated Ginger
- Oil for brushing

For The Yogurt Dip:
- 100g Greek Yogurt
- Handful Chopped Mint
- Squeeze Lemon Juice
- 1/2 tsp Icing Sugar
- 1 Green Chilli,finely chopped
- Salt and Pepper,to taste

Directions:

1. Place the flat plate in the grill and preheat on air fry at 200 C

2. In the meantime grate the cauliflower with a kitchen grater and mix with the rest of the ingredients until well combined. Form 4-6 balls and press them between your hands to form the fritters
3. Once the air-fryer has preheated open it and brush the flat plate with oil, then place the fritters on the plate and brush their tops with oil as well
4. Close the lid and cook for 5 mins, then turn the fritters over and cook for further 2-3 mins
5. To make the dip, mix all the ingredients in a bowl
6. Serve the fritters garnished with chopped coriander and with the dip on the side or drizzled over them

Nutritional Value (Amount per Serving):

Calories: 184; Fat: 8.36; Carb: 10.13; Protein: 17.61

CONCLUSION

An air fryer is a healthier alternative to deep-frying food and can be a creative way to cook a variety of healthy foods, including eggs, broccoli, yams, tofu, and potatoes in addition to meats and potatoes.

Using an air fryer instead of a deep fryer can cut down on calories, fat, and potentially toxic substances in your food.

APPENDIX RECIPE INDEX

Printed in Great Britain
by Amazon

16029004R10045